vaastu

A Path to Harmonious Living

v a a s t u

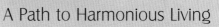
A Path to Harmonious Living

Lustre Press
Roli Books

Sashikala Ananth

This book is dedicated to my family – Raghu, Manu and Ahalya

who have been with me every step of the way.

ISBN : 81-7436-122-7

First published by Roli Books Pvt. Ltd. 2001
Lustre Press Pvt. Ltd.

M-75, Greater Kailash-II Market
New Delhi-110 048, INDIA
Phones: (011) 6442271, 6462782, 6460886
Fax: (011) 6467185. E-mail: roli@vsnl.com
Website: rolibooks.com

© Text: Sashikala Ananth

© Illustrations: Sashikala Ananth, Roli Books

Photo credits: Roli Collection, Usha Kris,
V.Muthuraman

Illustrations: S. Prabhakaran, K.P. Sudesh

Design: Yogesh Suraksha Design Studio

Printed and bound in Singapore

contents

many years ago, in one of the memorable talks given by J. Krishnamurthy, I was greatly intrigued by a statement made by him: 'Think with your heart, and feel with your head'. It seemed like such a whimsical thing to say, and if I didn't know him better, I could have dismissed it as a meaningless play of words. But I did know that Krishnaji was not in the habit of resorting to linguistic twists for effect; he was definitely pushing the listeners into a region beyond the frontiers of commonplace thinking, beyond the limits of conventional reasoning, and into the wilderness of unconditioned awareness. I was about seventeen or eighteen at that time, and my 'alternative' self was born that day. It is a part of me which occupies a very significant and central part in my personality today, but then on the first day, it was like entering an alien country and stumbling along on an uncharted trip. Much later on I picked up many such seemingly contradictory suggestions from various philosophers, Zen monks and Vedantic seers.

'Follow your heart, and you will know the right time to act.'
'No signposts adorn this universe of inner transformation. You have to become empty, for true change to take place.'
'In having abandoned himself to right action, Arjuna discovered the meaning of wisdom!'
'And King Ashoka stood on the battlefield and looked at all the dead lying around and knew that he could never hold the victory with complacence when the price had been so dear.'
'By pointing to the moon, many look at the finger.'

It was about this time in my life, when I was struggling to come to grips with my traditional roots and my contemporary training that I encountered the wisdom of the great thinkers from all over the world. Literally (and figuratively) my world came to a stop. I was propelled into another path, another reality, which accepts no domination of thought, which assumes nothing as being the last word, and where time does not move in a linear, logical pattern. I wandered into what seemed to be a cul-de-sac but did not come to a dead end, and which took me into many meandering lanes and through different journeys that have been both breathtakingly, achingly beautiful, and pitiless in their harshness. Out of this journey I have evolved many pearls of wisdom which have contributed to the richness of the world I now live in, and which have helped me in evolving a way of looking at the world that is anchored in the traditional world view and is yet so open and exciting that it can be adapted towards changing times with great ease.

The path of the reflective and intuitive mind
Till a few hundred years ago oriental philosophy was fairly consistent with the lifestyle of the people, and the individual could rely on the blending of philosophy and action in everyday life. The holistic

nature of thought, action, belief and assumptions made it possible to evolve a cyclical relationship between human beings and nature. But with the advent of colonisation, much of this shifted, and the dominant belief system of Europe with its great insistence on linear logic became the mode of transference of scientific thought and technological practices. Many debates have taken place in various forums to discuss this change-of-thought pattern. People like Swami Vivekananda and Sri Aurobindo passionately denounced 'mind colonisation'. But today, at this crossroad of one more change, when national boundaries are collapsing on the one hand and intense tribal identities are creating greater fragmentation in the other, which direction do we turn to? Many have told me that looking into the Indian past is a regressive action, and many others have tried to change me into believing that all Western thought is distorted and divisive. I believe that both modes of thinking and acting are relevant, and are products of great effort and contemplation of the human mind. What is required for us to do, is to integrate and blend the two minds – the rational and the intuitive – so that we may emerge more enriched and reflective.

The rational part of our psyche understands quantity very well, and requires empirical data to convince it of the efficiency of an argument. The analytical brain says, 'Give me proof that this is so; I cannot accept unclear statements or abstract speculations.' The 'scientific person' says: 'You must explain the hypothesis completely, and offer the parameters for your enquiry. At the end of the discussion, I must clearly understand the aim, process and end product.' All this is quite understandable given the nature of our lifestyle and the heavy emphasis given to materialism in the growth of the psyche. Manufacturers are demanding high profits and changing tastes are pushing them into marketing abstract ideas which are not always measurable. For example, 'fairness' is now a bottled solution! How does a consumer know when he is being taken for a ride?

The intuitive part of our consciousness is capable of comprehending the unstated and the unseen without requiring material proof. Listening to the commonplace utterances of a stranger, it is often possible to cull out the pain, anger, reactivity and listlessness that is not voiced. I have frequently reached out to strangers who were close to a breakdown, desperate for a human touch, and, perhaps, been of value to them, and all this in spite of no word being spoken out of the ordinary and the banal. This part of the human consciousness is a product of millennia of search into the imponderables of life, and cannot be dismissed as 'rubbish'.

This book is an offering to all those who have felt the urge to know and struggle with the many parts of their consciousness, without having to make a choice. This is for all those who would like to maintain their linear logic because it is useful and yet, live the inner life of the intuitive and the spiritual because it is more enriching and inspiring.

A view of Varanasi (Kasi). This particular view shows some of the unique features of this town, which have been retained throughout history in spite of endless rebuilding in the cityscape. Integrity of design relies on form, proportion, symbolism, material, colour and texture. Most of these aspects can be seen in traditional cityscapes.

the Pandavas stood at the edge of the land called Indraprastha and in their mind rose the city of their dreams with palaces, houses, market places, gardens, pools, temples and offices. The beautiful cityscape embellished with flags and *shikharas* of the taller buildings, the colours of the walls, the ornaments and sculptures on the *gopurams*, the coolness of the gardens, the wonderful fragrance of the flowers abounding in the pleasure groves, the bustle of a happy populace going about its business—all moved through the mind's eye of Yudhishthira. He realised this great dream with the help of wonderfully skilful architects and craftsmen. The *sabha* for the special functions proudly displayed glorious paintings on the walls, semi-precious stones glittering here and there, water bodies with lilies and lotuses, fountains and illusions of openings and steps. From this dream was created the marvellous city of Indraprastha whose great fame spread far and wide and is spoken of even to this day.

Descriptions of the marvellous cities of ancient India abound in the travelogues of Huien Tsang and Fa Hien. The *Puranas* refer to the cities of Kasi, Hastinapura, Ayodhya, Dwaraka, Kanchi, Vijayanagar, Ujjain and Lanka. The Tamil texts of the Sangam period extol cities such as Rameswaram, Madurai, Kanchi, Srirangam, Kaveripumpattinam, Chidambaram, Tiruvannamalai and Kalahasti. The beauty of the palaces, ornamentation of the temples, size of the roads with their street lights, shop fronts and aesthetic streetscapes are described in great detail. Settlement design and the allocation of facilities was an ancient wisdom and even today, some older towns boast of an order, aesthetics and spiritual serenity that these settlements exemplified. In spite of grotesque modern additions and unplanned extensions and changes in existing buildings, the atmosphere that prevails in the ancient cities and towns of Kasi, Kanchi, Tiruvanandapuram, Kumbakonam, Srirangam, Mysore, Kalahasti and Tiruvannamalai is extraordinarily uplifting to the casual visitor. This book is an exploration of the conceptual base and the physical manifestation of the great dreams of our ancients: this is an exploration of the *anubhava* or experience as it manifests itself into the physical field as *mano shilpam* or *mano rupam* (or the product of a mental vision). For the created form to be invested with the grandeur and beauty of the vision, it is important that many people should share the dream. The craftsmen, the designer and the builder must be evoked on the same wavelength. The occupants must comprehend and share the symbolism and the beauty of the process of creation. The collective space must reflect the ascension and the upliftment of the common dream. Every part of the finished product must hold within it the mysticism and the inspiration of the primary substance (*paravastu*). The connection between the part and the whole must endlessly sublimate the individual spirit so that it may eternally refine itself and bring to fruition the quest for the 'other'.

The connectedness, the order, the shared dream, the sublimation of the individual part, the keeping alive of the larger quest, and the constant shaping of the physical as it recreates the spiritual urges – these are all part of the Indian heritage. I have made an attempt to verbalise it in the journey through this book to discover the quintessence of traditional design.

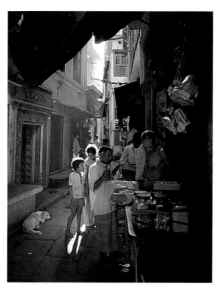

Facing page and above left: The Orchha palace near Khajuraho. The aesthetic balance of elements and the play of rhythm can be experienced in this building. *Above centre:* A street scene in Varanasi – the ambience is created out of light and shadow, form and stance. *Above right:* The sculptures of Khajuraho portray the eternal message of love and beauty to inspire the viewer. *Above:* Rajasthan – blending and adding the old and the new in a tapestry of time.

The Essence of Vaastu

the system known as *Vaastu* today was, till a decade ago, called by its full name *Vaastu Shilpa Shastra*. There were many subjects that came under the umbrella of *Vaastu Shilpa* and many more that are indirect to the main subject and yet play a very significant role in its impact and knowledge base.

Vas – to be, to reside
Vastu – matter
Vaastu – Residential space
or building

Vaastu consists of both the space and what is contained in that space. *Shilpa* refers to the form. Therefore, this subject traditionally dealt with all aspects of object-making and form creation. This included all types of buildings, settlements and villages or cities, furniture, chariots and other vehicles, vessels and containers, jewellery, swords and other implements of war, agricultural implements and religious and ornamental sculpture. There were five broad divisions in the community of the designers who dealt with the major activities listed above: they were the *manu* or blacksmith, *mayan* or carpenter, *twastha* or metal worker, *shilpi* or temple designer and stone sculptor, *viswagyan* or jeweller/goldsmith. There were many other groups of tribals and folk communities who handled other aspects of design such as costume, make-up, basket-weaving, textile-weaving, mask-making, pottery and many others. Almost all aspects of the needs of the

Facing page and left: Typical Rajasthani fort township. Culture and climate-specific concepts can be seen in Rajasthan in its flat terraces used for water harvesting and in the modular layouts.

community for implements, buildings, art work and craft were handled by traditional societies with great skill and effectiveness. Local materials were used, simple technology was adopted for the work process, the social system sustained the artists, and great ingenuity was employed in every level of the work, whether in the preparation of materials or the finishing of forms. The resulting designs were climate and culture specific. Then why is it that we moved into a blind imitation of Western-educated elitist designers to replace these indigenous systems?

There is ample evidence to show that the conquered races go away from their own strengths to imitate their conquerors, assuming that all they held in the past was dysfunctional. The 600 or so years of conquest has led the average Indian to this threshold of holding his/her past in ambivalence which is the product of a lack of connection between the older worldview and the contemporary view points of newer generations. A

The *Ratha* (chariot) festival. Thousands of devotees brave the crowd and the climate to participate in the procession. Celebrations and religious fervour mingle to create a unique Indian experience.

lack of dialogue, a frozen, unyielding position taken by elders, and the lack of social institutions to shape the growing minds into perceiving the holistic framework of traditional collectives have all led to the breakdown of many institutions and belief systems. Indian technology, which was the envy of travellers and historians till the fifteenth century, became atrophied and led to generations of Indians actually believing that science and technology originated from Europe. Today we are faced with the daunting task of having to bring together both the science and the technology of the tradition and to allow it to be led into a context which would catalyse a gracious integration between the old and the new. It is important to recall here that metal-making in India is one of the oldest and most respected methods in the entire world; the management of water sources is still an extremely viable method; excellent building processes and the employment of simple tools for achieving great tasks are still in practice; mathematical abilities and abstract patterning of the mind are an integral part of the Indian consciousness; the *panchangam* method of calculating the path of the heavenly bodies, which is one of the oldest in the world, is still accurate and valid; the quality of Indian textiles and the variety and beauty of Indian crafts are the source of national pride, and so on. Therefore it becomes extremely important that the subjects which deal with the various aspects of collective living that are explained by tradition be revealed to the world. *Vaastu*, in my view, is one of the most important subjects since it encompasses all aspects of community life, while also simultaneously plunging into the depths of the philosophy of *Vedanta*. It also has the added function of giving form to the sensuousness and innate artistry of the Indian psyche.

The anchors of design

The process of design is fairly similar whether the final product is a building, craft item, book, art piece, musical composition or any other. To achieve a balance between the finished product and what the *rasika* or connoisseur wants, the steps outlined centuries ago in the technical texts or *shastras,* in the inherited practices or *parampara* of the traditional artists / craftsmen, are still followed.

Process of design

1. The designing process should be based on a thorough understanding of the main principles and basis of design: *Bhogadyam* – functionality, *Sukha Darsham* – aesthetics and *Ramya* – the spiritual response to the manifested form.

2. The connection between the creative centre of the designer, the viewer / occupant and their experiences, and the form of

The *bali pitham* was originally used for actual sacrifice in the temples but today it is only an ornamental addition to the complex. But in the plan (given below) the *bali pitham* occupies a very significant location – that of the life energy of the cosmic being. The illustrations show two typical *bali pitham* from Tamil Nadu which have been designed with the same modules as the temple *vimanam* spires. They show the rhythmic interplay of line and form. **Below left:** Tirukkoyilur Trivikramasvāmi Temple. **Below right:** Mahabalipuram Shore Temple.

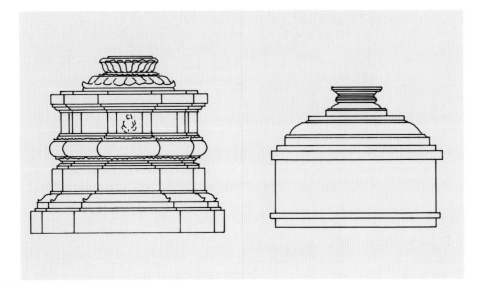

the designed object has to be coordinated.

3. The physical universe and the psychological one in which the manifested form exists, and the connection between these and the viewer / occupant needs to be worked out.

4. The impact of colour, shape, size, proportion of the object on the sensory perception of the viewer /occupant is important.

5. The well-being or inner harmony of the designer should be transferred on to the product and hence create 'healing' and 'repose' in the user.

This book elaborates on the fundamental principles of *Bhogadyam*, *Sukha Darsham* and *Ramya* with particular reference to the experience of space and form in the individual. The *atman* or spirit of the individual, along with the collective unconsciousness of the cultural system are constantly striving for an evocative ascension into deeper and higher levels of consciousness. In India the fine arts have been seen as a vehicle for offering this deeper evocation to both the individual and to society. The rhythmic steps or the grammar for this exploration have been laid out mathematically in all the traditional systems of thought and practice. There is also a lyrical, joyous outburst of sheer beauty which can be seen in the sculpture, architecture, poetry, music, dance and craft of every part of India. *Vaastu* is a combination of both the

A typical elephant motif. This can be seen in sari designs, terracotta wares, frescos, friezes (**see overleaf**), wall hangings, sculpture, pillar designs and craft objects. The shape of the elephant is beautified through the use of ornaments and fabric. The elephant is not only a realistic representation but also symbolises strength, grace and loyalty.

celebration and the grammar. This ability to hold together what appear to be apparently disparate elements of perception on the same plane is unique to Indian tradition.

Today the challenge lies in bringing about a synthesis between the philosophy, mathematics, spirituality and technology of the *Vaastu shastras* with the pushes and pulls of contemporary Indian society. Experiments carried out by societies who denied their past, failed to deliver solutions that can creatively bring people and nature together into a mutually enriching relationship. They have, in fact, proved destructive to the people and the environment. *Vaastu shastra* is capable of bringing about this integration, when seen in its entirety against the backdrop of yoga, *Vedanta* and ayurveda. It is important to study these four bodies of traditional knowledge for the human being to have a holistic understanding of his/her own environment.

Vedanta is the belief system and philosophy which gives meaning to life on earth, and to the seen and unseen connections between people and the vastness surrounding them.

Ayurveda is the *vignana shastra* or science of food and medicine which teaches a person how to bring about and sustain the essential balance of his / her own body.

Yoga is the *vignana shastra* or science through which the body/mind/breath may be balanced to attain the highest potential of personal energy in an individual.

Vaastu is the *vignana shastra* through which the *bhokta* or experiencer, and the built environment can exist in a dynamic relationship with each other.

Vaastu is, therefore, the manifested form which connects the belief system of a populace with the sane, healthy lifestyle it yearns for, and which offers it the inspirational ambience for deeper and more meaningful experiences. In this way, life can become more enriched. Indeed, we cannot undermine the importance of *vaastu*.

Left: Cave temple of Ajanta. **Above:** The splendour of a Khajuraho temple.
In a composite structure such as a temple or hall or city facade, many elements are juxtaposed to create a total effect. In the cave temples also such an effect was achieved by combining architectural features, sculptural reliefs and symbols from nature which conveyed a spiritual meaning through the compositions. Aesthetic pleasure was also provided to the viewer through the rhythmic interplay of form, space, light and shadow.

Vessels and utensils of various shapes and sizes for different utilitarian purposes, serve not only as practical and functional objects but also as aesthetic objects of beauty.

Bhogadyam
The Practical and the Functional

Long ago, in the city of Kasi, there lived a boatman who earned his living by plying his boat across the holy river Ganga. He would start his daily work after his morning prayer at one of the ghats adjoining the Viswanatha temple. It would take him several hours to get across the river since the Ganga, during the rainy season, extends as far as the horizon. On one such day, the boatman awaited travellers who desired to cross the river. Three well-dressed arrogant men came to him. One of them said in a haughty voice: 'Listen, boatman, set out at once. I am in a great hurry since I have to attend a very important ceremony.' The others added their impatient commands and the boatman pulled out his boat from the shore for the three men to get into.

A lot of time elapsed and the shore was left far behind. The city line of Kasi disappeared from sight but the distant shore on the other side could still not be seen.

One of the scholars turned to the others and said: 'I don't know if you are aware, but I am one of the most learned scholars in Kasi. I have studied all the texts and am considered an authority.' The next man said, 'I am a musician and am considered one of the best in this country. Many come to hear me from all over the world.' The third, not to be outdone, said: 'I am one of the richest men in Kasi. Even the king bows to me when we meet on the streets.' For sometime the three kept throwing their own greatness at each other but after a while their pomposity became monotonous, since all three kept talking and

nobody listened to the other. Finally they turned to the boatman, who was a simple man. Each one tried to prove his superiority. The scholar said: 'Have you read any of the great texts?' And the boatman replied very humbly, 'No, I am but an unlettered fool.' The scholar sneered, 'If you have not studied, then half your life has been wasted.' The musician then said to the boatman, 'If you do not understand music, then a quarter of your life has been wasted.' The rich man added, 'If you have not struggled and put aside great riches, then a quarter of your life has been wasted.'

The boatman remained silent. Just then a big storm arose and the boat was rocked by massive waves. Finally, when he could no longer control the boat, the boatman turned to his passengers and said, 'I am sorry, Sires, I am unable to control the boat any longer. There is nothing to be done except to jump and swim. I hope you will make it to the shore, since it is not too far off.' The three passengers turned terrified eyes to the boatman and said in one voice: 'But we can't swim.' 'Then your whole life has been wasted!' said the boatman and jumped into the water.

The above story is not without its lessons. The purpose of learning is not to show up how inadequate the other is. Whatever lessons one has learnt, however well one may have comprehended the mysteries of life, at all times, one must be prepared to tackle the practical and basic problems of living.

To live, one must be holistic in one's understanding. Actions cannot be completely successful unless the practical and the functional are also addressed. Sometimes sophisticated and complex edifices of thought and manifestation become dysfunctional because simple needs have not been addressed.

Bhogadyam : The functional aspect

It is said in the traditions of *vaastu*, that the basic needs of a building must be met for the design to be successful. This holds true for all crafted objects, be it a pot, a desk, a toy or a piece of sculpture. The basic utilitarian

An artist's view of a typical boat scene. This combines the practical aspects of boat-building as well as symbolism that pervades all of Indian art. The swan signifies speed, movement, grace and boldness.

aspects of the object must be understood and offered to the user. A pot that leaks, a desk that does not allow for comfortable writing, a toy that cannot be handled by a child, or a sculpture which topples over, are of no use however good the appearance may be.

The utilitarian aspect of design consists of two parts:

1. The designer must meet the needs of the user and be able to provide easy maintenance.
2. The design should be executed with materials that are strong, durable and easy to use.

In the traditional system of social connectivity, it was possible for both aspects to be dealt with by the designer and the manufacturer, since the entire operation was carried out within the family or community. Hence the selection of the material, the setting out of the design, the preparation and the completion were controlled by the group. It was in fact possible for the group to influence the sourcing of the material and monitor the waste. Till a hundred years ago, the carpenters were also part of forest conservation. (In fact their community held the knowledge base for forest management known as *Vana Samrakshana Samhita.*) They understood the origin of the materials, and had a great respect for natural systems. Protecting forests was definitely in their own interest.

User needs dictate design

All aspects of the design must be understood and provided for by the designer. This applies equally to technological innovations, craft objects, buildings or any other objects. A brief is set out by the designer which covers the needs of the user and it is out of these needs that a design solution is arrived at. Designers may operate in varied ways, but the basic criteria they look for are similar in nature:

1. The location of the building and the nature of the neighbourhood.
2. The rules pertaining to city development.
3. The budget and therefore the possible size of the building and the quality of finish.
4. The climate, breeze direction, light and ventilation that can be provided.
5. The rooms, activities, lifestyle that is required.
6. The philosophy of design that is being chosen.
7. The materials, shapes and colours that are being selected for the design.

Design methodology

Having established what the user needs are, the designer then proceeds to create a design, which satisfies those needs and brings out the creative potential of the designer.

Vaastu has offered several guidelines for the process of designing a building. The laying out of all the facilities is done after marking and allocating the grid on the land and locating the cardinal directions. In this way several concentric spaces are created, radiating out of the centre. These concentric spaces or *vithis/padas* as they are called, have a great bearing and significance in the ambience that is generated out of the design.

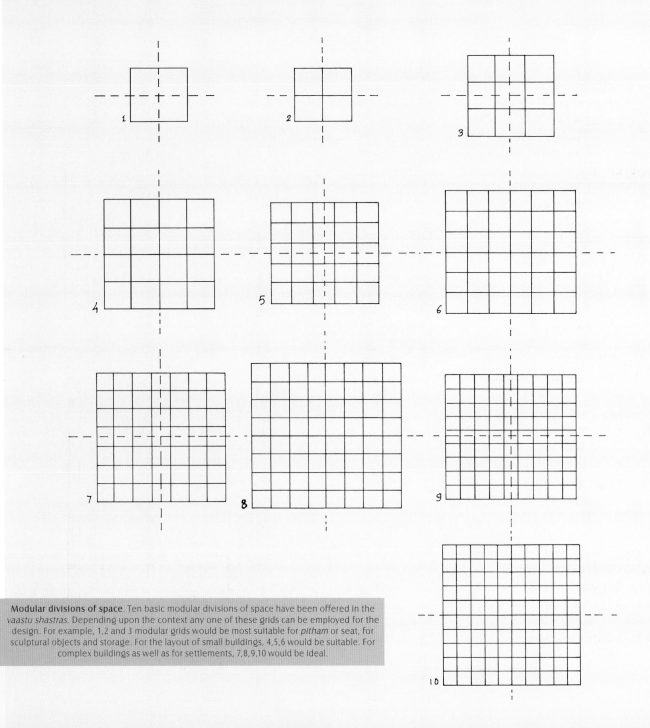

Modular divisions of space. Ten basic modular divisions of space have been offered in the *vaastu shastras*. Depending upon the context any one of these grids can be employed for the design. For example, 1,2 and 3 modular grids would be most suitable for *pitham* or seat, for sculptural objects and storage. For the layout of small buildings, 4,5,6 would be suitable. For complex buildings as well as for settlements, 7,8,9,10 would be ideal.

Pada vinyasa

Pada vinyasa is a method by which the given space is divided into modules. There are two kinds of divisions – the odd and the even. Each type has its own specific application. In general odd numbers of modules are employed for residential buildings, civic buildings and settlements. Even numbers of modules are used for temples, spiritual and community centres.

Brahmasthana
Brahma padam

It is said in the ancient texts that the centre of any *vaastu*, be it an individual building or a settlement, should be treated as the high energy point of the entire design. Therefore it is essential to either leave it open as a courtyard or as a quadrangle. Another option is to have a large room or building that is used as an assembly hall and which has ventilators at the top. When this central space is left open in a settlement, it can have trees or water. A religious building can also be located here. What is important is that the

Right:
Vithi or Pada vinyasa 1

1 Brahma padam
(Brahma vithi)

2 Deva padam
(Deivika vithi)

3 Manushya padam
(Manusha vithi)

4 Paisacha padam
(Paisacha vithi)

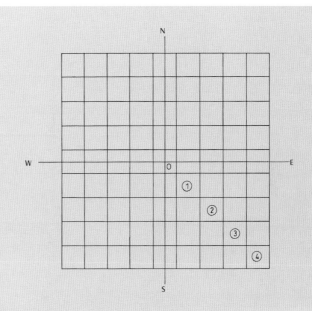

These two illustrations show two examples of how the space within a settlement can be divided. The two types of *vithi* or *pada* divisions signify levels of energy and the psycho-spiritual impact on the occupant.

Right:
Vithi or Pada vinyasa 2

1 Brahma

2 Ganesha

3 Agni

4 Jala

5 Naga

6 Yama

7 Kubera

8 Deva

9 Pisaca

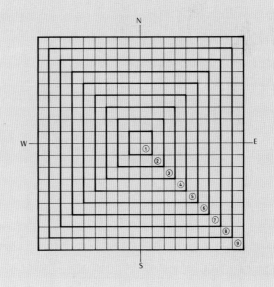

central point should not be stifled or burdened with pillars and walls.

Deivika padam

Around the centre is laid the next set of requirements. This space is considered to possess high energy and is, therefore, not suitable for individual activities in buildings or as the site of residential buildings in the settlement. The ideal use for *Deivika padam* in buildings would be for casual meetings and non-specific activities such as conversing or celebrating together in groups. This space is considered best for administrative, civic or educational buildings in the settlement.

Manusha padam

This space is suitable for residences, parks, water bodies, markets and business houses. In individual buildings this space can be used for all rooms in which any activity takes place – rooms such as the kitchen, bedrooms, dining room, puja room, and so on.

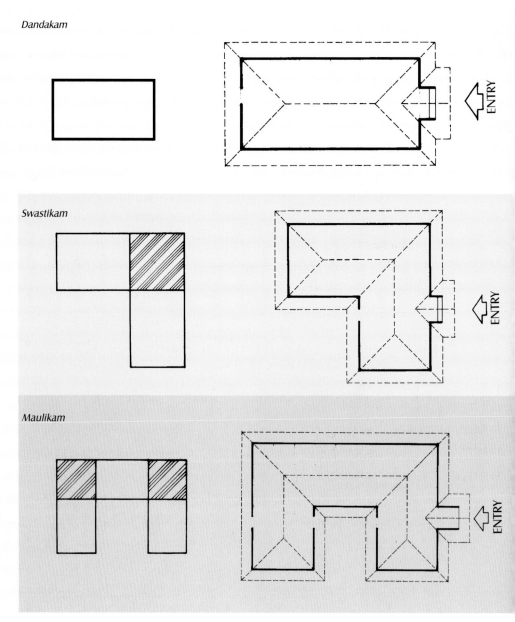

Dandakam

Swastikam

Maulikam

ENTRY

Chaturmukam

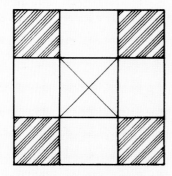

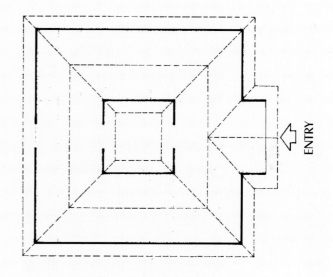

ENTRY

Sarvatobhadram

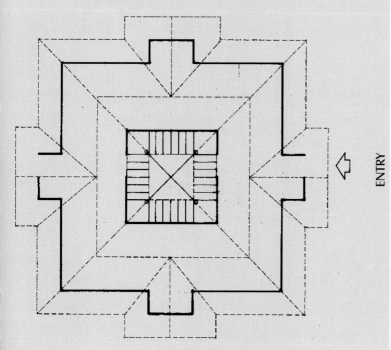

ENTRY

Building layouts. Starting with the basic rectangle known as the *Dandakam*, five types of building layouts have been recommended by the texts. *Swastikam* is composed of two *Dandakams* and one joint; *Maulikam* of three *Dandakams* and two joints; *Sarvatobhadram* or *Chaturmukam* has four *Dandakams* and four joints.
In the *Vardhamanam* (growth) any number of units can be attached together but always with a joint or verandah.

Vardhamanam

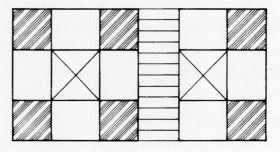

Paisacha padam

This space is also suitable for the activities mentioned in the *Manusha padam* in individual buildings (see p.30). It includes the outer roads, storehouses, manufacturing units, animal shelters and rest houses in settlements.

Shapes and designs

The six shapes that have been accepted by *Vaastu* as being suitable for design are generally implemented in different contexts. Rectangles are considered most suitable for residences. For schools, theatres and religious centres, squares are recommended. Polygons and circles are suitable for theatres, community centres and prayer halls. Triangles are considered to be highly difficult for use and are, therefore, recommended only for theatres.

Building materials

The materials that have been recommended traditionally are:
1. Stone, burnt or unburnt bricks, mud, and timber for the walls.
2. Timber, bamboo, stone for beams.
3. Tiles, thatch, shingles, slate and stone slabs for the roof.
4. Wood for windows and doors.
5. Lime, mud and a combination of the two for mortar and plaster.
6. Lime, mud and a combination of the two, stone and terracotta for the floor.

These natural materials are thought to be conducive for harmony and the well-being of the users.

Today, many types of materials are available which are artificial in their sourcing. To apply them in the building, one

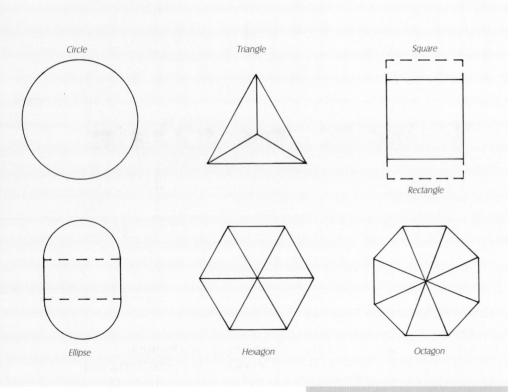

Circle   Triangle   Square   Rectangle   Ellipse   Hexagon   Octagon

Six types of shapes suitable for design

In most vessel and pot designs from different parts of the country, the practical or functional aspect is very cleverly blended with aesthetics. A most elegant line is combined with a user-friendly shape and the pot is easy on maintenance.

must think deeply about the relationship between the user's comfort and the impact on the ecosystem before making a decision. Overusing natural resources has its own problems. Using artificial materials creates a different kind of waste management problem. How then is a decision taken? Serious thought needs to be given to the question and sensible compromises have to be made so that the user is aware of the price the environment is paying for this consumption.

Creating an ambience

Mere location of facilities and choice of shape cannot offer a good design. It is absolutely essential to blend form, colour, proportion and aesthetics before the design can actually satisfy the complete needs of the users.

In craft items, the ambience that is created depends upon the user's ingenuity as well as in the flexibility of the item itself. Where settlement design and architecture are concerned, the designer has the freedom to define a user-pattern which would actually impact the lifestyle of the collective population. In traditional societies the design of a settlement was a product of decades of living experiences which slowly marked and influenced the environment with its own unique flavours. In India this influence of the design on the user, the lifestyle which emerged as a result of the use and which, in turn, influenced the ambience or design of the settlement as it grew larger, can be seen in varieties of locations. Let us examine the step wells of Gujarat which are probably the few living examples of what traditional societies felt about water and its place in society. Water sport pavilions and bathing houses have been mentioned in the *vaastu* texts but there are no living examples for us to understand the relationship between aesthetics and the practical needs that

Two views of the step wells of Gujarat. Though step wells are only used for the purpose of drawing water, the ambience created is extraordinary. The task of drawing water is done in groups and celebration of aesthetics and form becomes one of the primary tasks of *vaastu*.

governed the planning and design process of our ancestors. These step wells help us to understand this process.

There is a meaningful and specific relationship between the following :
1. Size
2. Shape
3. Proportion
4. Colour
5. Texture
6. Aesthetic elements

For the designed article or building to be understood as a complete *vaastu* experience, it is important that the functional, aesthetic and the emotional/spiritual aspects are in balance. Design is a matter of blending the size, shape, colour, texture, proportion and aesthetics into a manifested form that responds to the needs and desires of the user. *Vaastu* is the comprehensive method that addresses all these aspects, while retaining an essential connection with the culture and religious symbolism of a people.

Is it enough to address the practical and functional needs of people?

Tradition states that this is not enough. There is another need too: the design must offer food to the senses. Architecture must also be a sensuous and aesthetic experience.

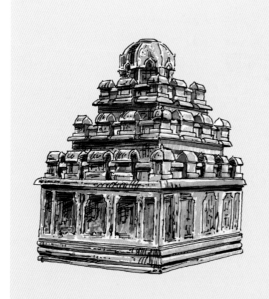  

Architectural elements from the Pallava period of Tamil Nadu. Simple shapes have been beautifully embellished. In the dagger **(on the extreme right)**, the mundane has been transformed by making the handle ornamental. In all the three examples, the basic design parameters have been very carefully adhered to.

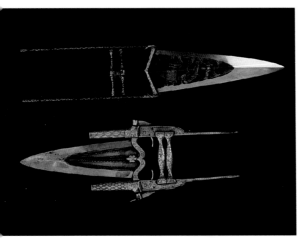

Facing page, extreme left (above and below): Intricately designed daggers and enamelled sword in Junagarh Palace Museum, Bikaner. **Above centre:** Typical *diyas* (lamps) of Kerala. **Above right:** A 1,000-wick lamp in Chettikulang Devi Temple in Alleppey district of Kerala – the largest temple lamp in India. **Right:** Traditional lamp with its symbols and aesthetic appeal.

Above, facing page and following page: Street scenes in Jaisalmer, Rajasthan. These show the aesthetic blending of form, projections, depression and the ambience that such an integrity of design can produce.

Sukha Darsham
Aesthetics and Sensuousness

traditional designers understood the urgent needs of climate, lifestyles, building materials and integrity of design. Their understanding led to the vibrant heterogeneous settlements of earlier times, so unlike the uniform sterile building settlements of the twentieth century. One such example were the step wells of Gujarat (see p.34). Another example is that of the desert town of Jaisalmer, which has integrated practical needs with the great beauty of the local craftsmanship.

The story of Mirabai as she yearned and desired for Lord Krishna to become a part of her being, is an exploration of the loved one as a part of the individual consciousness. Even as she was seeking the Lord in the temple, listening to His music in the garden, she drew closer and closer to Him within herself.

This paradigm shows that the search is just as important as the final integration – the process is as significant as the end result. The question is: Is the process of search only a dry intellectual discovery where every aspect is argued about? This may well fit the academic mould but the Indian love for poetry, colour, form and drama demands that the search be filled with the *navarasa* (the nine emotions which form the basics of Indian dance, theatre, poetry and music), through the pain of parting and the disillusionment of betrayal and so on, until there is a cataclysmic blending. Every time a story or any film made

and yet garner from themselves rare moments of greatness, reach extraordinary levels of sublimity and imbibe newer perceptions. In moments of great *bhakti* (devotion), Saint Tyagaraja would be so deeply involved in his music, that it is said that Lord Rama was there before him, listening to His devotee pour the quintessence of his search into the Lord's listening ears. At such times even if the King demanded the presence of Tyagaraja in the royal court, nothing would move the poet from his location, deeply connected as he was with His beloved. In fact, it is said that the King came to the poet's house at such moments to listen to the music and devotion in great humility.

Such outpouring of blessed connection with the larger consciousness can only be the good fortune of a few individuals. Other mortals can only participate in this celebration with grace and joy. For the individual then becomes one with a larger consciousness, the *Paramatman*, and we can only be a witness to this miracle.

Historical records frequently reveal that an inspired genius or an extraordinary soul is deified and the efforts made by this person to add to the collective consciousness are reduced to mystification and myth-making. One such example is that of the Konerirajapuram Nataraja.

In the great tradition of bronze-making of Tamil Nadu, the Nataraja image which stands at Konerirajapuram (near Kumbakonam) brooks no parallel. The image, without the pedestal, is 6' 6" high with a face of matchless beauty. It dates to the ninth century A.D. when the Chola kings were at the zenith of their power. To cast an image of this size and of such quality, the bronze maker would have required extraordinary skills both as an artist and as a technologist.

The popular story related about the building of the sculpture goes as follows:

Many centuries ago, during the rule of King Kandaraditya, Tirunallam or Konerirajapuram was chosen as the site for a temple to Lord Shiva. The King,

about the struggle of Mirabai to attain Her beloved, is read/seen, one not only empathises with her but examines one's own choices, meandering through our disappointments, joys and fortunes.

The power of the genuine seekers is their ability to be ordinary, vulnerable, mortal who was a great devotee of the Lord, wished to install a bronze Nataraja of unique size and beauty. He entrusted the job to his *shilpi* or sculptor and cautioned him as to its importance and the great need for innovation. This part of the story is factual. After this, in typical fashion, when faced with the complex and the technological, the legend becomes corrupted. It is said: 'The *shilpi* kept trying to make this wonderful image, and each time he failed. So he went to sleep in deep melancholy. In the night the Lord Himself came and drank the molten metal. It is He who is now enshrined in Tirunallam'. In their zeal to appear as great *bhaktas* (devotees) of the Lord, the scientific knowledge, effort, skill and the extraordinary teamwork of the *shilpi* group has been completely negated.

To cast a bronze piece of this size and quality the *shilpi* would have required 1 tonne of metal : Copper: 75-80 %, brass: 15-20 %, lead: 5 %, and gold and silver in minute quantities, depending upon the budget available.

Sculpture of Lord Nataraja. Tradition has placed the individual *liberatim* and the outer cosmic art of creation on the same pedestal in the form of the dancer. The dance represents the *jivatma* and the *Paramatma* simultaneously.

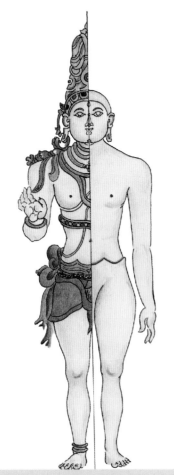

Sculptural image. This is a typical drawing made by the
shilpi with rhythmic modules for the laying out of the forms.
This is a *navatala* or nine-module form.

The other requirements would have been as follows:

The approximate quantity of beeswax would have been 100 kg.

The quantity of fuel required for the firing would have been 600 kg of coal and 2,500 kg of firewood.

The clay required for the casting would have been 100 kg.

The kiln in which this casting had to be carried out, and which would have been capable of handling the metal casting for such a large image, would have been at least three times the size of the finished piece. Ten to fifteen furnaces would have been required to simultaneously prepare the metal so that the pouring of molten metal was continuous.

A team of over fifty people would have been needed to complete this work. The time span spent in creating this masterpiece would have been at least one year. The size of the furnaces and the amount of fuel to be utilised for the process indicated that the workshop would have been located away from human settlements.

Sculpture and aesthetics

In the field of traditional sculpture or *shilpa shastra*, the aesthetics of the divine image played a very significant role in the life of the people. The *bhakti marga* or the paths of faith were enhanced with the qualities of the Divine One's characteristics being described and visualised in multiple ways. Poetry, sculpture, *harikatha* (storytelling with music), textiles, crafted utensils and furniture were filled with images of the beauty of the Lord and *Devi*.

Clothes and ornaments had a specific meaning both in the social context and in the emotional as well as spiritual context: the implements and vehicles of the gods offered to the people the capabilities and the skills of the gods as they protected, unveiled and transformed the mortal psyche. Lakshmi the consort of Lord Vishnu, was born out of the lotus which represents spiritual attainment. Lord Shiva holds His femininity as a part of Himself, and through this, He teaches His disciples to integrate the male/

female principles within themselves. There are endless stories and illustrations in this fashion, each part of the country showcasing images unique to its own history and *bhakti marga*. The beauty of Rama, Krishna, Buddha, Indra, Varuna is extolled in texts, helping the seeker to find the sublime in the search for beauty and excellence.

Grammar of design

Architectural beauty and sculptural beauty were part of the design brief of the traditional designer. It was not only the temples and civic buildings but even the residences of people, rest houses, schools and workshops that were beautified so that the occupants would feel a sense of sublimation as they went about their daily business. The basic element in aesthetics was the grammar of form-making or the mathematical rigour behind the making of form.

In the temple precinct, the image of the Lord or *Devi* in the sanctum was considered the

Sculpture form in flexion is known as *tribhanga*. Here too, the parts of the body are modular in dimension. Even the reduction in height due to flexion is rhythmic.

Facing page and this page: Images of gods and goddesses adorn the various architectural elements of a temple. They represent the universe of reality and are carved into the outer surfaces and the inner *mandapas*. but the *garbagruham* or inner sanctum is left completely unadorned since it represents the naked spirit in its cosmic womb.

primary measure. All the sculptural elements and architectural features were derived from this. The height or width or circumference of the image was taken as the primary module.

Let us say that the height of the image in a particular temple is H. This measure is a multiple of the face length 'A'.

$H = 9A$

The width of the sanctum is a multiple of H.

$S = 4H$

The height of the pillars is also a multiple of the height of the image.

$P = 2H$

The size of the *mandapam* would also be a multiple of H.

$M = 2S \ (8H)$

The height of the *gopuram* or entrance gateway and *vimanam* or tower over the sanctum would also be a multiple of this. It is usually referred in terms of size of the pillars.

$V = 4 \ P \ (8H)$

$G = 8 \ P \ (16H)$

A – face length of image in the *garbagruham* (inner sanctum)

M – width of *mandapam*

H – height of image in the *garbagruham*

G – height of *gopuram*

S – width of *garbagruham*

V – height of *vimanam*

P – height of pillar

H^1 – height of secondary image

The secondary sculptural images in the complex would also be in relationship with the primary image.

$H^1 = \frac{1}{2} H$ or $\frac{3}{4} H$

This is a simple extrapolation of the interconnection of measurement. In reality, there are hundreds of measurements that are derived from the primary module, and for this the traditional designer has many simple thumb rules for application which require mental arithmetic and great agility of calculation.

The interplay of form, shape, proportion, light and shadow can be seen in the facade of any temple. There is a variety of styles that have emerged in different parts of the country. In each of them, the juxtaposition of shapes, colours and symbols are specific to the location and hold great meaning to the people who inhabit the region. In fact, in some small towns, there is a fund of knowledge about the intricacies of design amongst the apparently 'illiterate' populace, while many of the 'educated' completely lack this wisdom. Perhaps in attempting to re-educate the people, we may be able to bring alive the connection between form and experience within the minds of human collectives.

Music, dance and other fine arts

Numerical games, arithmetic, proportions are all part of Indian fine arts. The evolution of ragas is based on the value given to certain sounds in the musical scale and the permutation and combination of these tonal locations. *Tala* is the rhythmic cycle into which music is placed, and there are scores of variations depending upon the ingenuity of the artist. Visual rhythm and the interplay of form is an important part of the exploration and struggle for the human being to connect with his/her divinity.

Above: A typical temple elevation.
Facing page, extreme left: Typical temple style of Orissa. *Facing page, left:* Temple of Khajuraho.

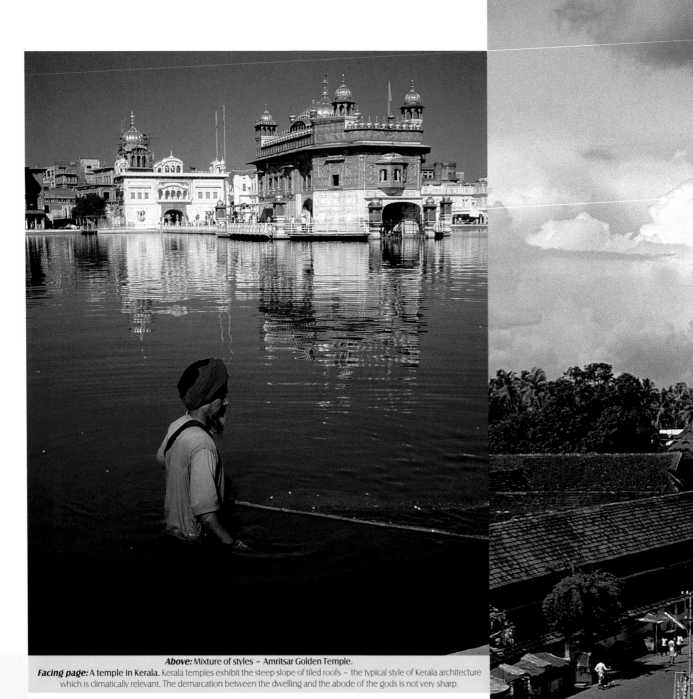

Above: Mixture of styles – Amritsar Golden Temple.

Facing page: A temple in Kerala. Kerala temples exhibit the steep slope of tiled roofs – the typical style of Kerala architecture which is climatically relevant. The demarcation between the dwelling and the abode of the gods is not very sharp.

Adornment, adoration

In the *rasa leela* and *nayaka* poetry and dance, the beloved is seen as the *Paramatma* and the lovelorn woman as the *jivatma*. The struggles of the individual in seeking and integrating with the larger consciousness is elaborately described in theatre, dance, music and the poetic traditions. In the temple rituals also this can be seen almost every day in certain temples, and on festive days in others. The image of the divine one is bathed, perfumed, dressed, ornamented, decked in flowers and jewellery, and finally all the people come and adore the form with their prayer and with their singing. At the time of the unveiling of the ornamented form, all the bells ring, the music and percussion rise to a crescendo, and the devotees stand before the sanctum shouting their fervour. It is said that at this time the *Paramatma* enters into the hearts of the *bhakta*.

In theatre also, the procedure for preparing the being (*patra* or vessel) of the actor into the character he/she is playing, is an elaborate ritual, sometimes taking as much as six hours. At the end of it the actor is supposed to let the spirit of the character enter into himself/herself. This emptying and filling up of the consciousness has a certain rhythm and order given to it which is very close to the rhythm and order of iconometry and temple ritual. The drone and deeply hypnotic movement of the percussion instruments is a very important part of the ritual in both cases.

The place of sensuousness, festivity, ritual and exaltation are slowly being eroded in our search for modernity. We seem to be divesting life of all its drama and excitement and making it sterile and monochromatic. Can we discover the joys of group celebration and the mystic nature of spirit calling in our collectives? Spiritual calling, celebration and lamenting are essential parts of the human yearning for the 'larger' and the 'divine'. Can this yearning and the need for rationality coexist? This is the foremost pressing question to be addressed.

Ramya
Spiritual Harmony and Inner Poise

Long ago, in a small village on the outskirts of a great kingdom, there lived a sage. His ashram was devoted to the preparation of disciples who were walking the path of self-realisation. There were many students studying with him at different levels of personal evolution and he was well known for the unconventional tests he carried out to measure their inner growth. One day he called all his disciples and gave each of them a *laddu* (Indian sweet) and said: 'Eat it where none can see you', and sent them away. Each of the students pondered and responded according to his own interpretation of 'someone and no one'. One of the students hid behind a tree where the sage could not see him and devoured his *laddu*. Another ran into the forest nearby and ate his share; yet another crouched behind a haystack to eat his *laddu*. One boy climbed to the top of a tree to eat; another descended into a pit to eat his, and so on. After a few hours, the boys started to come back one by one and each one shared with the master his own ingenuity in finding a place without people where he had eaten his *laddu*. Some had hidden from animals while others had even hidden from birds and insects. The master was pleased. The boys had exhibited great forethought in the exercise. Finally, the last of the boys came

Ratha or temple chariot. The structure of the chariot is a miniature representation of the temple *vimanam*. It exemplifies the principle of *jivatma* and *Paramatma* or the subtle substance within the human being and the cosmic substance, respectively. While the chariot is the form of the cosmic Being, the image within is the spirit of the Being. The chariot that is pulled by people through the streets symbolises the mobile personification of the spirit that guides all human beings while living in their midst. This spirit lives with and within each person.

Ornamental lamps. In these two examples of ornamental lamps , not only is there proportion and symbolism but also the employment of mythology to create a spiritual awareness. The images may be of gods and goddesses or of playful human forms which are copied from temple sculptures.

back, and he still had his *laddu* in his hand. The master demanded angrily, 'Could you not find any place to eat, you silly boy?' And the boy said very simply, 'Wherever I went Master, God was watching, and I could not escape Him either in the forest or in the hill yonder. I found nowhere to hide from His all-seeing eyes. I am sorry I could not carry out your request'. The master was greatly moved by this, and it is said that this boy was groomed to become his successor in the ashram.

This story illustrates the innate harmony between the inner self and the divine or cosmic energy that surrounds all of us. When each of us becomes aware of this harmony, then the interconnection between all aspects of creation is constantly perceived. Achieving a balance, rhythm and the discipline of inner and outer realities becomes a sacred task for each of us. The *Vaastu shastras* describe this balance between the inner space and the outer form of a building as the primary goal of architecture. To make this

possible *vaastu* has introduced the concept of *ramya* or spiritual well-being. There are several ways in which this can be achieved. Let us look at a few of them.

Pada vinyasa

The site or physical space is divided into *vithis* or *padas* that are concentric spaces around the centre of the site. The centre is known as the *Brahmasthana* or the energy centre. All other facilities are laid out around the centre. In residences the centre is the courtyard or open hall. The rooms are placed in the outer rings. In settlements the centre is the maidan, temple (religious building) or sacred grove/water.

Ayadi poruttam

After the design has been worked out the linear measures of the building or settlement should be checked against what is called *Ayadi poruttam*. By this method the benefits of the building/settlement can be fine tuned. There are either six or eleven types of tests for the measure called *shadayadi* or

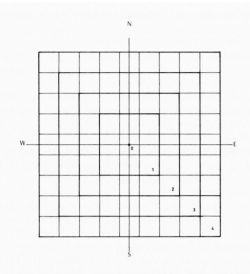

N

W —— E

S

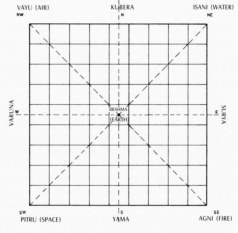

VAYU (AIR)
NW

KUBERA
N

ISANI (WATER)
NE

VARUNA
W

BRAHMA
(EARTH)

SURYA
E

SW
PITRU (SPACE)

S
YAMA

SE
AGNI (FIRE)

1 *Brahma*
Padam

2 *Deivika*
Padam

3 *Manusha*
Padam

4 *Paisacha*
Padam

Left: *Pada Vinyasa* and
cosmology

Below: *Manduka padam:*
8 X 8 = 64 squares;
Paramasayika padam:
9 X 9 = 81 squares

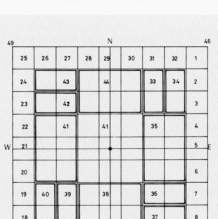

MANDUKA MANDALA
(8 X 8 = 64 squares)

PARAMASAYIKA MANDALA
(9 X 9 = 81 squares)

1	*Isani*	26	Naga
2	Parjanya	27	Mukhya
3	Jayanta	28	Bhallata
4	Indra	29	Soma
5	Aditya	30	Arga
6	Satyaka	31	Aditi
7	Bhrsa	32	Diti
8	Antariksa	33	Apa
9	Agni	34	Apavatsa
10	Pusa	35	Aryaka
11	Vitatha	36	Savita
12	Grhaksata	37	Savitr
13	Yama	38	Vivaswan
14	Gandharva	39	Indra
15	Bhrnga	40	Indrajit
16	Mrga	41	Mitraka
17	Nirrti	42	Rudra
18	Dwarapala	43	Rudrajit
19	Sugriva	44	Bhubhrt
20	Puspadanta	45	Brahma
21	Varuna	46	Charaki
22	Asura	47	Vidari
23	Sosa	48	Putana
24	Roga	49	Paparakshasi
25	Vayu		

shodasayadi. This practice is an ancient one and is still commonly in use.

Inner radiance

When the rhythm and proportion are perfected, can it be said that the design is timeless and exquisite? In yoga it is said that the regulating of the breath, the perfect discipline of body and movement and the stilling of the mind lead to great equanimity. But above all this, it is said that the being should be filled with the light of wisdom for a transformation to be complete. But though the preceding steps can be practised, the last one of luminosity can only happen through *anugraham* or grace. In *vaastu*, I have found that this step into timeless beauty can happen when the designers and the designed form are in perfect equipoise and the context receives the design with great tenderness. The inner radiance can only be a spontaneous result that cannot be planned or wished for. It is definitely the result of 'grace' or *anugraham*.

There was once a farmer who had three sons. He had vast lands and plenty of oxen. The farmer wanted to give his great wealth to the most creative and ingenious of his sons, so that he would know how to use the wealth for better purposes. He called the three of them and said, 'I am giving you one rupee each, and these three empty rooms. Each of you must fill up one room to the best of your ability with the money given to you.' (Needless to say the story is set in the distant past when the rupee had greater buying power!)

The first boy went to the nearest town and bought one rupee worth of hay and filled up the room. The father was pleased. The second boy bought one rupee worth of sand and filled his room. The father was pleased with this too. The third boy bought a small mud lamp, a piece of cotton, some oil and a match box with the rupee and lit the lamp inside the room after dark. The light filled up the whole room. The father was thrilled with this and said to the third boy, 'You will be my successor, for you know both

Above: Pedestal and shrine design. This is a beautifully designed pedestal as well as a small shrine. In this all the symbols have been suitably employed so that the entire composition affords the *bhakta* many ways in which he/she can attain liberation.
Facing page: Theyyam dancers in Kerala. In this form of ritualistic dance the preparation and community participation in the ritual is very high.

The horse *(above)* and the swan *(left)* have been adopted in various architectural and sculptural contexts as symbols.

thrift and innovation. Look after your inheritance with caution on the one side and ingenuity and creativity on the other.'

This is a most inspiring story that takes us to the edge of one kind of understanding and pushes us into another dimension of learning. To keep probing within the perimeters of only one dimension of understanding may not always provide the answers. It is sometimes required that we move beyond the realms of belief and knowledge of one field to be able to discover something 'new and innovative'. To achieve this is not easy. What is required is concentrated attention and the ability to empty one's consciousness so that something entirely new and different can take its place and be absorbed.

In yoga, one of the types of meditation that is practised requires the *sadhaka* or practitioner to sit near moving waters (whether it be an ocean, river, waterfall) and meditate on the sound until all sound ceases inwardly and in the silence, something different can be

The lion *(above)* and *makara (below)* are used in various concepts as symbols.

Above and facing page: In jewellery too, symbols are employed for aesthetics as well as for refining the spirit.

perceived. This creative impulse comes out of abandoning oneself to the sound, and then freeing oneself from it so that something unique and creative can be unlocked.

Symbolism – states of consciousness

The final aspect of the rigour of design is that of a commonly held idea of aesthetics and symbolism. This would correspond with the shared beliefs held by people regarding life and death and a life after death, and the dialogues among human beings, nature and the guardians of various levels of consciousness. This part of architectural symbolism and the meanings of form and space are unique to the traditions of India. This includes the pantheon of the gods, the deification of the environmental energies, the eulogising of phenomena, the stylisation of natural forms, the constant connection between cosmic happenings and human destiny and the fascination with the occult. It also includes the preoccupation with rituals and prayer, the importance given to

yoga and the honing of the spirit, and the holistic connection between context, people and time. All this and more form the metaphors for the manifested designs of the tradition. Let us examine a few of them.

Each symbol (see pp. 62-63) has clear and definite meanings and interpretations based on the culture of India. The symbol of the horse depicts speed, grace and beauty; the swan depicts

uniqueness, beauty, faithfulness and discrimination; the lion stands for power, aggression, authority, domination and solitude; the *makara* denotes dissolution, new beginnings, confusion and integration.

By and large symbolism in Indian architecture and sculpture performs the function of motivating and inspiring the individual towards the sublimation of the human spirit.

Facing page, above and right: Traditional Indian beauty manifested in the timeless elegance of the sari. In many communities the sari itself is seen as a complete universe, with the 'body' of the sari known as the earth *(bhumi)* and the shawl of the sari as the sky *(akasha)*.

Poornam
The Part and the Whole

there was once a guru or teacher whose fame spread far and wide for his unusual teaching methods. Students came to him to be initiated into a different process whereby they could examine life and not merely receive instruction.

One day one of the *sishyas* (disciples) came to the guru for his daily lessons. The guru, in his wisdom, felt that the student was ready for a challenging and evocative shift into another realm of consciousness. So when the student said, 'What will you teach me today, Master?' he said, 'I want you to find out what you need for your survival.' The student, who was used to the strange ways of the guru was taken aback with this mundane question. He replied, 'Sir, I require food, clothing and shelter to survive. Out of these, food is the most important element.' The guru asked him, 'How will you find food?' 'By begging for alms, as is our custom.' 'If you were in a forest with no one around?' 'I would look for natural food such as fruits, berries, roots, nuts and others.' The master then said to him: 'Go into the forest and

Facing page and left: Chennakeshwara Temple. This temple style abounds in rich ornamentation and sculptural marvels.
Above: Chidambaram Temple. One of the earliest temples, this is a temple town dedicated to Lord Shiva the dancer, and is a symbol of *akasha* or space.

gather your food for the day.' The boy went and looked around the forest and came back with a collection of edible stuff from the forest. Then the guru ordered, 'Find the food at night', and the boy went out on a moonlit night and gathered his food. He was next asked to find his food on a moonless night and he did this by finding his way around in the starlight.

Then the guru sat very quietly for a while. After a few minutes, he looked up at the boy and said to him: 'Up to now you have done well. Tell me now, boy, what would you do if there was no light at all?' The student thought for a while and then said, 'I would use my other senses to find the food: my nostrils, my hands, my ears and my tongue would be my guides. Above all I would rely on the power and sensitivity of my mind and inner intelligence to find what I need. I realise that beyond the senses, there is a sharper and more reliable intelligence within me.' The guru was satisfied and praised the student for his great sensitivity.

The concept of wholeness or *poornam*

The Brahman *is infinity or wholeness; the* jivatman *is also wholeness. From that wholeness has this wholeness come. When you take out* jivatman *from* Brahman *what remains is still whole (or infinite).*

In *vaastu* or building design this concept can be restated as the connection of *vastu* and *vaastu*. The form of the substance is *vastu*, the space within the form is *vaastu*. For example, gold is *vastu* and a vessel made of gold is also *vastu*. The space contained within the vessel is *vaastu*. Mud is *vastu*, and so is a mud bowl *vastu*, but the space within the bowl is *vaastu*. The movement of form into space and space into form is

Facing page: The *garbagruham* or sanctum where the deity is housed. **Left:** In Buddhism the image of Buddha or any of his relics is placed in the sanctum.

interconnected. Within the mind of the designer there is an imaginary form and space known as *mano vastu* and *mano vaastu,* respectively. The potential manifestation of this form is known as *mano rupam* and *mano shilpam*. When this form is manifested in the outer space as a sculptural object or building, it is known as *shilpa vaastu*.

The five stages of design

1. Environment or context of the building
2. Impact of the design on the occupants
3. Interconnection between the manifested form and the environment
4. The external quest of mankind to comprehend the meaning of life, death and the origin of creation, and the connection between the built form and the quest
5. The psyche of the designer/s

The first two stages are *bhogadyam*, the third is *sukhadarsham*, the fourth is *ramya* and the fifth is the consciousness of the Creator. When all five steps are integrated, then the design is capable of satisfying the users in different layers of their consciousness. Such a building is called *poornam* since it represents the entire creation in a small scale. It is also capable of leading the psyche and spirit of the occupants into the complete experience of the individual spirit which is again called *poornam*.

Universe of *vastu* and *vaastu*

On the earth many elements or *vastu* exist, each containing

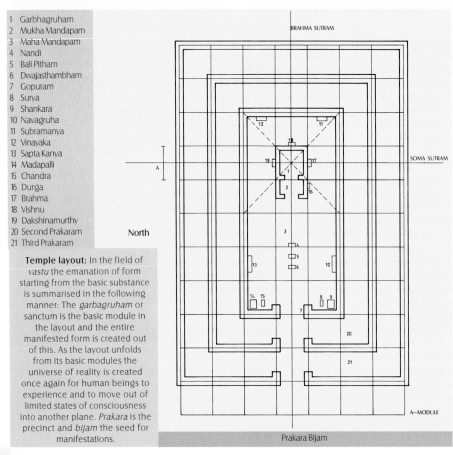

1 Garbhagruham
2 Mukha Mandapam
3 Maha Mandapam
4 Nandi
5 Bali Pitham
6 Dwajasthambham
7 Gopuram
8 Surya
9 Shankara
10 Navagruha
11 Subramanya
12 Vinayaka
13 Sapta Kanya
14 Madapalli
15 Chandra
16 Durga
17 Brahma
18 Vishnu
19 Dakshinamurthy
20 Second Prakaram
21 Third Prakaram

North

BRAHMA SUTRAM

SOMA SUTRAM

A—MODULE

Prakara Bijam

Temple layout: In the field of *vastu* the emanation of form starting from the basic substance is summarised in the following manner: The *garbagruham* or sanctum is the basic module in the layout and the entire manifested form is created out of this. As the layout unfolds from its basic modules the universe of reality is created once again for human beings to experience and to move out of limited states of consciousness into another plane. *Prakara* is the precinct and *bijam* the seed for manifestations.

vaastu or space within. Human beings are also part of this and the earth too is a *vastu* while the cosmic or universal space is *vaastu*.

Surrounding all substances is the primary space. In the Indian traditions of thought which is known as *Vedanta*, the individual substance and cosmic space or intelligence are known as *jivatma* and *Paramatma*, respectively.

The *jivatma* is composed of the same material as the *Paramatma*. The human mind is *vastu* just as the Divine or *Paramatma* is also *vastu*. But within the mind there is a great emptiness or *vaastu* and this creates matter or *vastu* continuously.

The *Paramatma* is the primary *vastu* and *vaastu*. This intelligence or *Paramatma* which has different levels of *buddhi* (discriminative intelligence), *manas* (mind), *ahankara* (ego) continues to create all the time.

Jivatma or intelligence which also has levels of *buddhi, manas, ahankara,* also creates.

When these two levels of

A Khajuraho temple. In the *mandapam* of a temple, the width and height of a pillar, the ornamentation on the pillar and the openings in the walls are all rhythmic with the size of the sanctum.

creativity are rhythmic with one another, they offer contentment. This whole process of design and execution in *vaastu* is akin to creating congruence/ alignment in the individual form as well as in the settlement.

The process of manifestation of form

Vastu is the primary substance that contains the promise of the final form known as *rupam*. The latter comprises both the outer object and the inner substance. When it is only in the mind it is composed of the

mental traits of the person concerned but when it is placed in its physical context, it becomes integral to the physical system.

The designer begins by absorbing the impetus of the outer challenge within the mind and from this, he/she creates mental forms known as *vastu*. Out of many such *vastu*, the psyche of the designer creates the final form *(rupam)*. The psyche is also *vastu*. The *vastu* of the building and the *vastu* of the designer are part of an on-going and simultaneous interaction.

The design process takes place

within a design context. The substance of the designer's mind interacts with the brief given for the design. After a great deal of inner activity, the designer comes up with a form within the mind. This is known as *mano vastu*. Since this form too contains vibrant space within it, it can be concluded that the mind of the designer creates both space and form that are in response to the pushes and pulls of the context.

Mano vastu (energy)

↕

Mano shilpam (form)

↕

Mano vaastu (space)

The interactions in these three stages of creation are the source for the manifested form. The field or physical space that is called *vaastu* is undifferentiated and limitless. Into this the potential of the designer creates and places form that is known as *shilpa vastu* and the space that surrounds this object is *shilpa vaastu*.

The final form is then placed in its context, and in its turn, becomes the field for other activities and processes to take place. Therefore the process of creativity can be stated to begin with substance and end with substance.

The action takes place in a field and finally emerges into a field. The basic tenet of *vaastu* can be stated as the emergence of manifested form from the subtle space of the mind. The manifested form in turn becomes the space from which other forms and spaces can emerge.

In the process of laying out the individual house and laying out the town or settlement there are many interesting concepts that are stressed in the *vaastu*

A village plan

A Maidan or open space, religious centre

B Offices, schools

C Residences, temples

D Markets, residences, temples, travellers' lodges, medical centres, workshops, animal shelters, water bodies, wells, tanks, where necessary

A village on the outskirts of Jaisalmer, Rajasthan. Many principles of *vaastu shastra* can be seen in traditional layouts.

texts. Let us take the example of Tiruvannamalai: each part of the town has been located in a specific way with strict adherence to its vibration, its energy and its form. In Tiruvannamalai the entire settlement upholds a discipline and order both physically and psychologically. The Tiruvannamalai *muzham* or scale was employed to set out the whole town. The shrines on the outer periphery of the town follow the *vaastu purusha mandala* or modular diagram with each *lingam* dedicated to the *deva* (deity) in that specific place, such

as Varuna *lingam* in the west, *agni lingam* in the south-east, Yama *lingam* in the south, *vayu lingam* in the north-west, Isani *lingam* in the north-east, Niruti *lingam* in the south-west, Kubera *lingam* in the north and *surya lingam* in the east. From within this location each element brings in its own characteristics for the well-being of the people. *Agni* is the energy of the fire; Yama is the energy of death and rebirth; Kubera, of wealth; Isani, of nurturance; *vayu*, of intellectual power; Varuna, of adventure; Niruti, the power of ancestry;

surya, of knowledge. The part and the whole are never in isolation but in consonance.

Two kinds of simultaneous movements are essential:

1. A movement from the outside into the centre, which cleaves through the *koshas* (the psycho-spiritual sheaths of consciousness) into the still centre which is alive with the potential energy of creation.

2. A movement from the inside which starts from the point and moves outward into universal phenomena.

There are counter movements

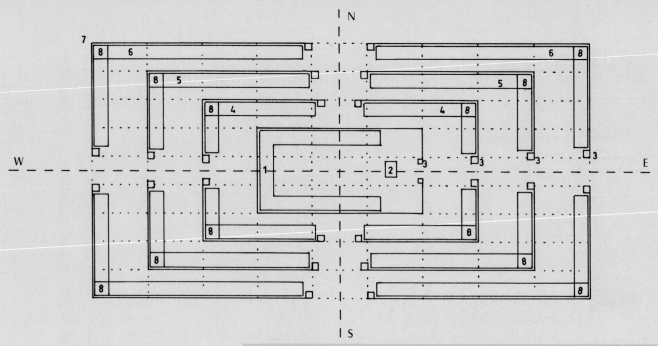

Above: A traditional layout of a town. The town has a palace in the centre and an open space in front of it. The other facilities are placed as per the recommendations of the text.
Facing page: Umaid Bhawan in Jodhpur, Rajasthan. In a traditional building the central hall is frequently raised with openings from the top to provide light and air to the entire complex.

into the individual centre and the rhythm of outer order.

To achieve such a harmonious balance between the smallest part and the larger whole, several steps have been set out in the *vaastu* tradition.

a. The smallest module should match the derived measures of the following:

(i) The *nakshatra* or moon sign (according to Indian astrology) of the client;

(ii) The length of the thumb of the client or *karta*;

(iii) The *nakshatra* of the deity;

(iv) The *nakshatra* of the town or settlement.

b. Every room reflects the larger pattern.

c. The centre must be open; it must be space or *akasha* within which the point can exist without oppression.

d. In an individual building this is the courtyard or living space. Out of this space the other needs are created.

In general the centre of a settlement can contain sacred water, space, grove/ tree.

1. A temple or religious building, and/or meditation hall may be placed in the central module but it should be set back from the central point.

2. The next concentric *pada* can have offices, residences and even include rooms for administrative purposes.

3/4. The next two concentric

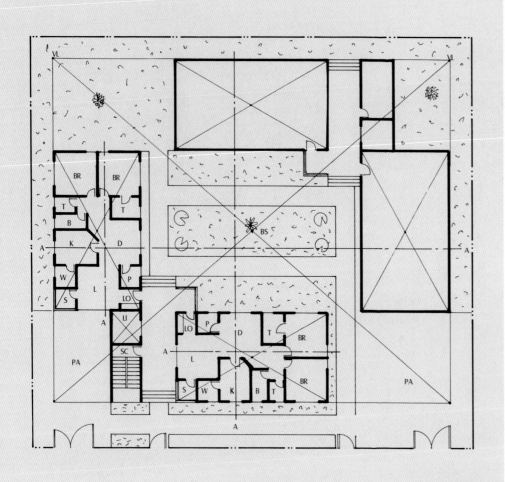

VL = *Vaastu* limit
BS = *Brahma sthanam* or centre
A/A = Central axis
PA = Parking area

BR = Bedroom
B = Bathroom
K = Kitchen
D = Dining room

W = Washing area
S = Study
L = Living Room
P = Puja room

LO = Lobby
LI = Lift
T = Toilet
SC = Staircase

Block of 16 flats
Ground floor
First floor
Second floor
Third Floor
Module E:- 14:8

A contemporary high rise designed by the author with a large quadrangle in the centre and flats all round

padas can have residences, with some administrative offices and shops.

5. The outermost *pada* can have residences, bazaars, security offices, travellers' lodges, hotels, eateries, entertainment centres, hostels, religious shrines, congregational spaces, craft sheds, service stations, gardens, recreational areas and exhibition pavilions. This part can be larger than the others (2 or 3 modules width). Larger bungalows and manufacturing units can also be located here.

Whatever be the nature of the settlement, mixed or specific activity-based, the layout must reflect this quality through measurement, material, colour, form, layout and integrity of design.

It is also essential to locate the building with a larger quest in mind. The layout of an individual building in an open space and the layout of different buildings in a settlement create an overall pattern that affects the minds of the occupants. Therefore, it is

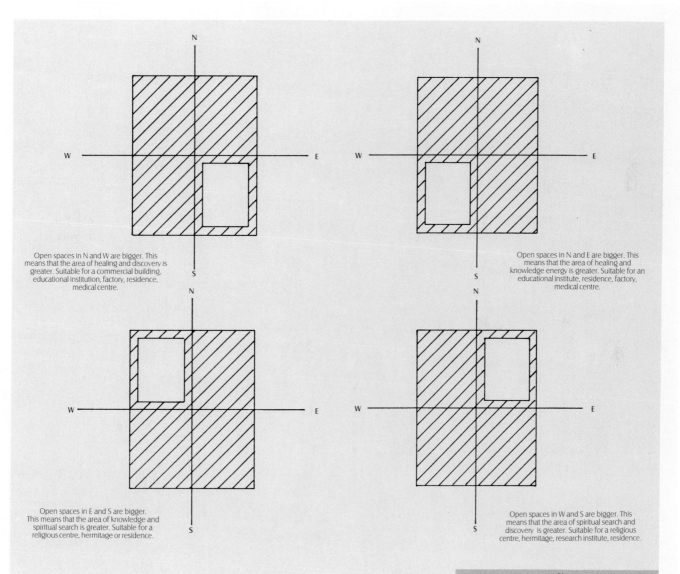

Open spaces in N and W are bigger. This means that the area of healing and discovery is greater. Suitable for a commercial building, educational institution, factory, residence, medical centre.

Open spaces in N and E are bigger. This means that the area of healing and knowledge energy is greater. Suitable for an educational institute, residence, factory, medical centre.

Open spaces in E and S are bigger. This means that the area of knowledge and spiritual search is greater. Suitable for a religious centre, hermitage or residence.

Open spaces in W and S are bigger. This means that the area of spiritual search and discovery is greater. Suitable for a religious centre, hermitage, research institute, residence.

Four types of layouts

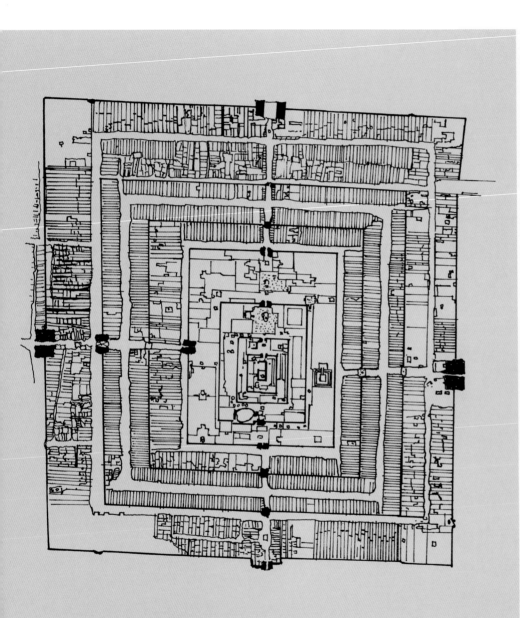

Layout of the town of Srirangam. A temple town, Srirangam has five concentric spaces in its layout which become progressively wider on the outside. This is an excellent example of *prakara bijam* in application.

essential to remember that design, space, designed objects and people must be in balance and harmony with each other.

Though the outer form varies in the various temple styles in India, the core concept of design, wherein the *garbagruham* in the central space is treated as the preliminary module, is common to all styles. The measurements of all elements in the layout are consonant with the image in the *garbagruham* and there is a grammar of form and meaning within which the ornamentation is placed. This helps the devotee to traverse his/her inner world and ascend into nobler heights. This methodology is common to all temples. There are a few thumb rules that have been adopted in the tradition, which may be employed in the layout of settlements even today.

The concepts of *vaastu*, with its focus on mutual connections, is a valid design methodology which has universal application. The designer and his/her creativity, the space in which the designed object will be placed, and the interaction between object,